THE FADO HOUSE

First published in 2012 by
The Dedalus Press
13 Moyclare Road
Baldoyle
Dublin 13
Ireland

www.dedaluspress.com

Copyright © Mary Noonan, 2012

ISBN 978 1 906614 57 7

Dedalus Press titles are represented in the UK by
Central Books, 99 Wallis Road, London E9 5LN
and in North America by Syracuse University Press, Inc.,
621 Skytop Road, Suite 110, Syracuse, New York 13244.

Cover image 'Juggler and Tightrope Walker' by Duncan Grant.
© Estate of Duncan Grant. All rights reserved, DACS 2012

The Fado House won the 2010 Listowel Writers' Week
Poetry Collection Prize, sponsored by Profile Developments.

The Dedalus Press receives financial assistance from
The Arts Council / An Chomhairle Ealaíon

THE FADO HOUSE

Mary Noonan

DEDALUS PRESS
DUBLIN, IRELAND

ACKNOWLEDGEMENTS

The poems in this collection have appeared in the following
magazines and anthologies: *The Alhambra Poetry Calendar
(2010); Best Irish Poetry 2010; BigCityLit; Blackbox Manifold;
The Captain's Tower: Seventy Poems for Bob Dylan at Seventy;
The Cork Literary Review; Cyphers; The Dark Horse; The Echo
Room; The Listowel Anthology (2010); The Moth; Penned: Zoo
Poems; The Same; The SHOp; Southword; The Stinging Fly; The
Stony Thursday Book; Tears in the Fence; Wasafiri.*

CONTENTS

5

For my father, Pats,
and in memory of my mother, Marie

Now it is a long time to the Feast of the Assumption,
When my mother will come

To collect me in her pony and trap
And we will go calling on all our cousins
And take tea and sherry in their parlours.

—Eiléan Ní Chuilleanáin, 'The Crossroads'

Keep Talking, Babe

It was his dream to see me through a screen
With words and music and a cast of dwarves
Playing card-sharps, hecklers, fire-eaters.
My only act was to jabber, but I could work it up
To a howl, and this I did for centuries.
The beauty of my inflection was enough to catch
The crowd, and when I had them I'd lunge
Between whisper and rant, spinning on plosives.
Sometimes, to keep myself warm, I'd do my dance
Of the one-legged crow, toppling against the glass
As walk-ons bared their teeth and catapulted me
With pennies. Only the voice could stop me.
'Not now. But tomorrow. Keep talking, Babe. Keep dancing.'
And I would do my questions – always the same –
Is he near? Did he see me pinned? Did I suffer good?
How do I turn off these eyes?

I Will Gabble

No matter my dream of you will not –
you rang, out of the blue I was tumbling about
moiling as usual the phone stopped me in my tracks
I had long since stopped believing in a world
that could take my breath away but there you were
phoning and asking to meet me for lunch
such a small thing, for me, a miracle, asking to meet
me, still shaking from the shock of seeing you
in the street after one of our eight-year intervals
the lop-sided smile, the mystifying eyes, the bulk
of you just one big question-mark I wanted to file away
under 'to cry about' and then you rang, caught me
on the turn in the stair, dogged in my belief in an earth
bent on its predictable axis, I in my runnel, pecking
and scratching for ever and instead I was picking up
the phone and there you were my heart ripped
from its coat of mail and tap-dancing all over my chest
and no matter I will gabble and you will look at me as
at something you couldn't make up and no matter
my dream of you will never – you rang.

Phone

Will the black rain never leave off
                              its lashing?
There's snow in the north-west,
fishermen are drowning in the east.
Not even my Japanese blanket can keep the
                              heat in me.

Won't you reach, easy-peasy, for
                              the phone?
I see you, clasping your glass
of Roussillon red, delving into the dust,
singing a song about a diamond that wants
                              to be coal.

What passes through that skull of yours –
                              the rattle of me?
The ping? Uncurl your fingers, set me to
baking apple-upside-down cake, walking the roadsides
for a hedgerow bouquet of snowdrops latticed to
                              wild fern.

Swallow

Sprays of red haw tell her it's time
to go, and she's springing from thorn,
feathered back brindled with sprigs
of damp straw, soft throat soaring free
of snagging bramble, winging south
over blackberry and furze. She has met
with nothing here but rain, the kind
of rain that flushes mountain ash
and chestnut from clogged earth.
Roadside hedgerows bow as she glides,
fuchsia lanterns flop to damp ground.
Soon she will be darting over miles
of dust track, past ghost shack and scrub,
glancing off rock cacti that do not sink roots
but run feelers lightly over dunes, cup rain
as it slides through spines.

Evening in Muscat

for Claire

On the beach at Seeb, fishermen land 'hammour', 'king fish';
an old man in tattered sarong sits in a stoneware sink
washing his feet, cold water flushing the body's grime
with the guts of the morning's market.

The muezzin's cry rings from unseen minarets, incantatory,
unavoidable. Cushions and satellite dishes litter flat roofs,
wind chimes scatter flocks of small parrots.
Cocks crow, night falls quickly.

In the Sultan's plant nursery, turbanned Indian workers
see to the final tasks of the day, cluster under stars to watch
a television set, rigged to corrugated sleeping sheds.

On palm-lined tracks, fluorescence begins to flicker:
carved intricacies of doors caught in the glare of neon;
the smell of jasmine flowers on warm night air.

Damascene

A bunch of tiger lilies
and damask roses in deep green
and I am mended, braided
in blankets of attar, all fraying
stemmed in the eye of a flood-tide
threading city streets with eels, otters.

Night Traffic

for Matthew

That December night, she raced down the unlit path
to the frost-covered gate, shouting to him to hop across,
to duck and dive in the traffic and he called back that he
ran the risk of being flattened by cars, by the black stream
flowing between them. But the rush-hour and the dark
and the shouting and the wind and rain were not enough
to run him, with his two bags, into the next parish
and he landed in the yellow hallway, in the bright kitchen,
brushing sleet from his jacket and dust from a bottle and
words into the oak of the table. Into the candle-flame went
talk of Mexico City and the high-wire circus of Budapest
and the German outposts of Transylvania and the lure
of pepper (chilli, paprika) and three bottles of French wine
and the touch of his hands. Stepping from the taxi now,
she looks across at the icy gate, at the blacked-out eyes
of the houses beyond, glimpses a flickering presence
peering too, pondering the plunge into night-time traffic.

At the Zoo

He took me mainly to places of leave-taking –
Bahnhof Grunewald (Auschwitz, Belsen),
the grave of Heinrich Von Kleist at the Wannsee
and airy galleries hung only with paintings of death –

pulled me, running, through the tunnels of the S-Bahn
as if our lives depended on some west-bound train
we were about to miss. But the aquarium stopped us
in our tracks, we spent hours there, days

pressing our faces against the icy violet jellyfish
gliding on their eddies and back-draughts,
their silken root threads quivering to pulse-waves,
pulling against the vortex. Clasping cold fingers

we would eye the hybrid lives of the zoo –
feather-toed hens, dwarf donkeys, kangaroo-rats –
and dream a stampede of roaring ghost animals
in the Tiergarten, on the run from the trains.

The trees in the zoo's park were still frozen
in their early bud, pushing small flowers into air
full of the mewling of unseen birds. Snowflakes
falling on the Spree were tiny gulls.

The yellow U-Bahn took us home, its bulbs rocking,
pale petals fluttering in the arc of its headlamps.

Persephone

Saint Brigid's Day has come and gone
and I am unbound from my tomb, adrift
in chambered earth, listening for sounds –
dull drubbing of dryads in leaves,
twitching of bone-dry twigs, dripping
of ice-water from rock.

But nothing moves in the earth above
my head. I feel the dull weight of trees,
mute prisoners on a hill, hacked back
for new growth. The sad machinery of Spring
has not yet begun its slow picking open
of cauterised hide, letting pistils weep again,
feel the palsy of frost-scarred stem.

From my grave I look upon the crucified forms –
rags of sycamore against a mouse-grey sky,
stumpy limbs of butchered lime, claws of ash
frozen in their grasping at air. All is waiting,
feeding on the food of the dead. What hope
for us, rooted in Hades, unfurling,
forever opening our palms

to Demeter's elusive touch, reaching to the mother
who cannot save us now, did not save us then,
when we set out across the field of flowers?

But I Should Never Think of Spring

after Hoagy Carmichael

You brought a ghost with you, her prints
in the softening earth, her snowy breath
on the windowpane, on the mirrors, but mostly
clinging to the air between us, to our lips,
to the voice of Hoagy Carmichael as he sang
I Get Along Without You Very Well – you didn't
know his music but fell when you heard that, saying
you had never heard such a song, saying you wanted
to hear all his songs, your eyes full of soft rain dripping
from leaves, your voice full of sheltering in her arms.
I lay beside you and listened, looking into the dark eyes
of the fox, the dark eyes of the owl and Hoagy singing
It's not the pale moon that excites me that thrills
and delights me oh no it's just the nearness
of you, the nearness, you listening for a name,
or someone's laugh that is the same.

Frida and the Monkeys

after a painting by Frida Kahlo

Frida sits on the veranda of her blue house,
eyes fixed on the giant orchid poking
from a stone jar before her. The flower
is a buttery yellow, its fleshy outer whorl
enclosing an ochre throat striped with ruby –
the mouth of a cave lined with tiger skin.
She sits, bolt upright, her broken spinal column
clamped in a steel corset that spikes her ribs.

Two favourite spider monkeys squat
on her downy forearms, their long arms
stretching round her shoulders, wizened
hands cupping the back of her neck.
Their mouths are fixed in a solemn moue,
their black eyes, like hers, stare at the plant.

Sounds of a band break over the wall.
The monkeys twitch and flick their tails
at red cactus flowers, sleeping parrots
leave the shade of the jacaranda and flap
at shuttered windows as kettle drums
and shrieking cornets lead a frayed gang
of clowns and rope-walkers into the alley-way
beyond the house. Frida cannot see them

but she knows them, knows the double-bass,
the little bassoon and the big bassoon, the oboes
and green ivory hunting-horns, the bagpipes
and fipple-flutes, knows the caterwauling,

the banging on her ear-drums, knows the dwarf
woman, her perfect woman-sized feet kicking
and stomping and jerking the band forward.

Frida closes her eyes, opens her lips
her mouth, her ruby throat. A howl
ricochets off the garden wall, scattering
monkeys in trees.

Eduardo's

In a restaurant made from the thin arms
of a tree embracing a white-washed room,
I eat strips of duck and strands of almond
prepared by a stooped Belgian gentleman.
A wall of glass separates me from him,
and within this wall swim miniature
tropical fish, all black and red stripes,
mother-of-pearl and orange polka dots.
The fish and I go eyeball-to-eyeball,
the tip of my nose touching
the bumpy nodules atop each flat face
and the gauzy fins billowing
and flicking as they whirr past my ear,
up and down the watery wall.
I dive into a Douro red and the flashy fish
and the silver-haired gentleman and I swim
into and out of each other. He slices pink duck-
breast and flambés raspberries in vodka
and the thin brown arms of the tree squeeze
us closer and the chalky fringe of the low ceiling
blanches the top of my head.

The Fado House of Argentina Santos

The women here are of a certain age
        their doubles hang in black and white
on the walls – photos showing
        the wailing women of 1930s Lisbon
hair set in bird's nests, eyebrows
        pencilled.

The ancient doyenne, queen of the *fadistas*
        sits in her lair by the door
a hawk in navy blue.
        From a serving-hatch framed in *azulejo*
her elder sister peers. Faithful retainer
        in black and *broderie anglaise*

her task is to fix lace doilies
        in bread baskets. And spy. Not a word
passes between her and the others –
        middle-aged *meninas* spilling
from worn needlepoint bibs, pinned in
        by tight bows at the waist. Nightly

        they dance

their angry fandango on fallen arches and varicose veins
        battling, in the time between *fados*,
to get tubs of *bacalhau* down to the trestles
        where the drunken tourists wait.

On the half-hour, lights are flicked off
        a silver-haired *fadista* steps from the shadows.
Cradling herself in a fringed shawl

she opens her throat and ululates
in broken tremolo for the old dreams, for Lisboa

for what was lost.

And her frilled serving-sisters stomp
the dough-white flesh of their calves
and scowl.
And Argentina Santos watches from the door.

Rua João das Regres

The green neon of the Hotel Portugal
lights the end of a narrow street
where a king once entertained
his courtesans. Nowadays, poor women –
young and old, fat and thin – are enshrined
in the street's doorways, down-at-heel
madonnas haloed by shop-signs for
Cape Verdean antelope, shawarma,
a barber's, a knife merchant's.
In the Praça do Figueira, a bronze king
balances atop a high marble column,
keeping his eye trained on India, a gull
nesting in his crown. A young woman
runs at a drunk, flinging a bucket of flower-
water over him, his body hitting the ground
with a slap. By night the prostitutes slip
and slide on unsteady pins over wet tram tracks
as the yellow 28 beetles down from Alfama,
its driver jerking the gear stick, jamming the bell.

Muse Manqué

In the poem, I will not be leaving
tyre skids on the drive as I whoosh
away, nor will I have vampire eyes.
I will not be shedding my snake's
– or my lion's – skin, to take again
my woman's form, nor will I be wood
or stone coming to life at the touch
of your hand.

In the poem you will write, there will be
no green, no ghostly girl beckoning you
from the Red River shore, no face
in the dust, no drowned princess.
Nor will your skeleton have to trawl
the sea-bed to find the pearls
that were my eyes. You will not be
stretched out on my grave.

In the poem you will write for me
I will not be joining the women behind
the locked door of your blue castle,
nor those parked in your box of blue
paint-brush women. What will I be?
What will I be? Will I be Mata Hari –
Hotel Aviz, Lisbon, 1915 –

arriving in a flurry of feathers
and palm fronds, with rings
on my fingers and bells on my toes?
And will I be contrary,
the long-awaited-much-desired-

double-trouble-centre of your operations,
key to the submerged vault from where
you hoist your maps and codes,
your lost women?

Visitor

What are you, bloated white face louring
one eye dragging, black mascara running

mouth down-turned – poor clown – can I help it
if your nerves are shot to pieces can I stop

your face from dripping on the floor or folding
behind black clouds can I stop your demented trooping

your circling of the globe, looking, looking
your eternal waxing and waning, pushing and dragging

the weight of the world's waters in your veins?
I used to know your every phase

could chart your flitting through the houses of the sun
but now your full-blown face catches me unawares

takes my breath away each time with its pouncing
as if from some childish hiding-place or hollow.

You are older than Mount Olympus, why come here
pressing your face against my window? You can still

haul me in, make me shiver at your icy radiance
the silvery shoals moving across your skin

but soon your snowy face, blasted and pining
for Heaven knows what, will let fall its frozen tears

on someone other than me.

Household Plant

Countless plants, budded under a bad star,
came to terminate their existences here,
drying and shrivelling in undersized pots, starved
for want of a look, the brush of fingers on stem or leaves –
until *this* turned up. A cutting from an optimist,
it sits today in the self-same pot in which it arrived,
fruit of eight winters of disregard, feeding on dust
and what light it can glean from my northern window.

After several years, its foolhardy persistence
caused me to take a second look. It grew.
Each May it would stop me in my tracks
by springing its pendant flowers on me,
pearlised stars, small and slight as snowflakes
glistening on a fantail of dark foliage –
showers of brazen spade leaves flashing
black velvet to the light, deep red to the shade.

Mesmerised, I would sit and look, wanting
to stroke the silken teguments, each with
a green eye at its core, fine thread veins radiating
to pink-speckled stems and all sprawling wildly,
a luxuriant Medusa on the mantelpiece,
luring me to wonder at its resolute cycle,
its blatant refusal to wilt, its snatching of life
from thin air, from the stones housing its roots.

The Card

What goes by the name of love is banishment,
with now and then a postcard from the homeland.
—Samuel Beckett, *First Love*

I'm looking for a card,
one that holds the oriole
on the black pear tree –
will it be brazen or sweet,
June bug or whippoorwill,
Tupelo or Baton Rouge?
I drape myself in maps,
drift in colours and signs,
sleep on my seven books
of owls, frogs, alligators.

I want a card that quickens
codes, spills the secrets
of words, sends letters flying.
We used to name things,
now we travel the lines
past ghost-shack and scrub,
sun-bothered lizards skittering
under creosote and ocotillo.

This card must distil the frenzy
of the firefly as it waltzes
with its own blazing corpse.

At Beckett's Grave, Cimetière Montparnasse

A metro ticket bears the inscription 'What are we waiting for,
    Sam?'
A warm breeze, ruffling the sand in the avenues,
carries an answer, light, like leaves: *We have time to grow old.*
The air is full of our cries.
An acacia bends over his grave, shadowy fronds
dancing on the marble.

Walking past *Le Dôme, La Coupole,* I think of him,
and of the time when all of Paris packed
these Montparnasse *dancings* to hear big bands
play the Biguine, the Rhumba, the Java –
artists blowing the sale of a painting on champagne,
city bodies surrendering to the scandalous rhythms
of the Caribbean.

And then I see the spindly frame hurrying
from under the tower of black glass,
late for his rendezvous, with Giacometti,
maybe, and murmuring, as he clips along,
his voice a marmoset on his shoulder, that
all is falling, all fallen, from the beginning
on empty air.

Herald

i.m. Albert Serceau 1993–2007

How did the tawny owl get into my dream?
A speckled ball of fluff, rusty orange and white,
with an oval white head and yellow-flecked
black eyes, tumbled in, flitted and dipped round
the room, light as air. Children were there,
trying to catch him in their fists, and when
I called out to them not to squeeze him
to death, he slipped through their fingers
and was gone.

Two months later I see your face
on the mortuary slab. You are wearing
your red bandana and your yellow sweat-shirt.
Your favourite Barbie is keeping you company.
What are those purple marks on your cheek and nose?
Your body is jagged, frozen in its last attitude,
your dark lashes resting on your round white face,
the brown eyes you used for talking sealed now
beneath their lids. I imagine your smile

remember the owl small enough to fit
in the palm of my hand and the children circling
round him, trying to grasp him, and the heart
beating in the ball of feathers as he slipped
through their fingers.

Learning to Name

for Daniel

Your first word is crow.
Kwoh, kwoh, kwoh spilling
from gourd of belly to small mouth
and out, sounding a dark octave in air.

You meet yourself in this squawk
and you meet others, seen in trees
or gliding in straight flight,
compact, hooded, sleek.

The bow of your throat sends notes flying,
you caw your first song of love
singing the strangeness of you, of them,
your nape silver, swathes of indigo
billowing

until black letters fall and you call raven,
rook, jackdaw, chough to the cave of your voice.
And they come, ragged pall-bearers,
despised peddlers of sorrow.

Seagulls in St Andrews

They come to the hotel window each morning
on the dot of seven. Like ghastly choristers
floated in on the *haar*, they dangle in the crack
at the top of the closed curtains, wailing –
that is how I am woken in this town where a storm
swooped and made off with the roof and ribs
of a cathedral, leaving a sandstone nave
to sail the firth, a bone-white baptismal font
to brazen it out on the foreland. Along the road
lies the witches' lake, where women were flung,
thumbs tied together, big toes tied together –
if they swam, they were fished out, fed to a bonfire.
The salt-cured trees could tell a tale
of neat crofts, pared gables, hangings.

Island

The day we went out
to the island the wind
was a gale force eight.
The swollen waters pressed
at the prow of the ferry
with a portion of the Atlantic
in its hold. The boatman
bounced on his seat as he steered us
to moor in the rift
between the black cliffs.
We walked the island's spine,
three miles from end to end
and we met not a soul, the wind
so high we had trouble keeping
our feet on the heathery moss.
We didn't think to lie down
and watch the white clouds flying.

A lone, red-footed chough
commanded a granite outcrop,
gulls struggled to move
in the air above our heads.
Driven back to the hotel,
we sat on the edge of the bed
eating Irish cheese
and drinking French wine and gazing
at the picture framed in the small
window: a meadow of long grass
billowing in waves
and swallows darting, touching

the tips of the blades and springing
off again, unconcerned
by the wind's raving.

Perfect Day

Do you remember the day? It was
the best day of the summer –
best day of the year – the day
we had all been waiting for
since the start of time and when
it came round I found myself walking
alone on the edge of a horse-shoe bay
on a northern beach where even
the sand was blue, shimmering
like the sea with the reflected pastels
of the sky. Families and lovers were strolling
as in treacle, their movements made slow
and fluid by the heat. Smells
of barbecued meat and sounds
of children squealing were carried
on the breeze, three horses cantered
in the shallows, their fetlocks lapped
by small waves. Swallows were diving
in the long grasses
doing their bed-time acrobatics.

Do you remember the day? It was
the best day of the summer –
best day of the year – the day
we had all been waiting for
since the start of time and when
it came round I found myself walking
alone on the earth's rim as the sun
slowly eased itself into the warmed-
up Atlantic and a long letting go
of breath rippled across the waves

and the dunes and across the chests
of the lovers and mothers and fathers
and boys and girls holding hands and
playing and picnicking on the beach.

Carry

To clear my head of talk, I walked the beach
and found a pebble, a cuckoo's egg,
held it and saw it was a map.

An oval stone striated with slate-grey markings,
one side bears tracings that arch and criss-cross:
polka of narrow roads,

sandpipers darting in bleached grasses,
contours of a shoreline, the lines on my palm.
A gate opening into a small field.

The curve of the stone offers concentric swirls:
a talisman to ward off the evil eye,
or the nipple of a breast.

Here it is, an amulet, runes and traces
to light and guard you, a cuckoo's egg
in the wrong nest, a gate opening

into a small field, a circle ploughed
round a lone hawthorn tree, a map
of the way between us. I carry it.

The Limits of Radio

When I travel, a silver Yacht Boy radio
is my sole companion,
signalling the world, transmitting
me over oceans, deserts
sealing my raft

in concentric circles of static and babble.
But Yacht Boy cannot
save me from you, from thoughts
of how I might capture you
in waves

net you in short frequencies.
The needle spins
along the bands, swivels to the north,
to the east, picking up Armenian, Portuguese,
Arabic

and mermaid turbulence.
Where you are,
only the rasping of electrical storms,
the rattle of hulls and blanched bones,
hiss of lungs

filling with white noise.
Is that you I hear,
faint, as you sink
beneath the sedimentation of voices?

No Direction Home

i.m. Gregory O'Donoghue 1951–2005

I wrote that the final days of August would find me
washed up, propped in a place where the light of day
is tight and mean. You approved, gently tending –
even poems lamenting summer's end were safe with you,
lines too concerned with the small ambit of seasons
to encompass the impact of a true ending.

And so it was that August swept you off your feet,
quenched your breath with ease as she dragged
hurricanes and swollen waters in her train.
In the middle of your fifty-fourth year –
one of the bald facts mourners swapped at the grave,
suddenly aware that they did not know you.

I knew only the grace of your yellowed fingers,
that elegant pen, your hand feathering its tender script
across a page, your hooded eyes, your mug of gin,
the small room where we met once a week.
I saw you sometimes, walking lopsidedly in the street;
once, at a launch, we talked about Bob Dylan

but in the moment I heard of your death I knew
that you had guided me to a place – a room, a page –
where limping and stammering come into their own,
a vast, airy space inviting me to stand my ground,
to bellow in tantrum, to rampage, to thrive
in my brokenness.

The Rosslare Train, Fermoy, August 20, 1956

for my father

I was spiked yesterday at the Mardyke summer sports,
my bare foot crushed by a well-shod runner
on the finishing line. Running barefoot, I ask you,
on the eve of emigration! I heard a woman say
'He's had a heart attack', and I laughed –
my heart is sound as a bell.

The foot slowed my departure, though.
I had to have it bandaged today at Mellerick's Chemists.
I was sitting in the snug with my leg on a stool
and whatever look I gave at the window
I caught a glimpse of you, in your lemon box jacket
and your polka-dot skirt to the knee.

I saw the sun on your dark hair, and on
the determined line of your cheek and jaw.
Marie. Will I ever see you again?
I know now that if I travel the world I won't find
another woman like you. I'm making my journey
with a shadow heart.

As I limp to the top of Barrack Hill, suitcase in hand,
I look back on the town, and on twenty-eight years.
The best years are gone, you said. It's true this place
couldn't give me a living, but it gave me running
and leaping and playing – a wild boy's life.
What lies before me? The building sites,
the boarding-houses. My heart not sound as a bell.

Lone Patrol

You told me about him. The small horse
is one of your memories, the few
remaining, a barrel of a two-year-old
who burned himself on your inner eye
in the 40s and never left, galloping round
the inside track of broken recall,
a colt crouching under a ditch by the Bride
for two winters, then racing, unbeaten
in bumpers, over hurdles, over fences
with Sean Hyde on his back, a Raparee
ranging over the rough courses of the South
in the days when horses were bought
and sold for a song. Your father paid
a Mrs Watt for him in the Grand Hotel
and there he was. Tramore, Listowel
Limerick Junction, you with your father,
your main man, the two of you travelling
the race meetings of Munster together –
you   will   never   forget   him –
the rough and ready days of mud,
three-card-tricksters and tic-tac men,
and you making a book with your father
in the rain, always the rain. Lone Patrol –
sent to England in the end, there was no
future for him here, the stocky body
weaving in the sharp bends, the low frame
steady in the home strait, lone scout
holding the line, but too small
for the steeplechase at Market Rasen.

He broke his back, the sentinel
who still patrols your lonesome fens
and borderlands.

Bright Day

i.m. my mother

There is a sea of people
in the church. The ceilings are high.
I have made the long walk
to the golden railings on my spindly legs
in my white Communion shoes and socks.
The crowd pushes to the big swing doors.
Outside it's a bright, bright day.
The white sun flashes at me and I want
to fall, the cough I was keeping
at the back of my throat starts to bark.
My mother looks at me, at my white face
at the black rings circling my eyes.
She has a question on her face.
She stretches out her arm, her hand
cups my elbow, her other hand clasps
my wrist – helping me across the road.
The sun's daggers are flicking
at cars as they pass. My spiky elbow
rests in my mother's cupped hand,
in the soft pads. Her roly-poly fingers
press through the nylon of my white
summer cardigan, the elbow folds
into the blanket of her hand.
From elbow to wrist, she holds the long bone,
carries it across the road.

No Shoes

As a child I would sit at your feet,
stare at the flame ciphers on your snowdrop legs –
you said they were ABCs – and wait to hear
how the fire had crooked its long fingers at you
when you were seven, soldering cotton to starved skin.

Nuns bathed you in egg-whites,
dead grandmothers waved from the chimney,
greedy to see if you could flower again
from the albumen pod.
A seared corolla I knew only in story.

You were ashamed of your feet,
the bark skin you hacked with a scalpel,
never wanting to press heels in sand,
let toes unfurl to the life of water.

At last, you asked me to wash them –
a disciple's duty, the awaited gift of touch.
I cradled tapered lilies, petal teguments intact
since the day of that Communion photograph.

Others came to wind the body,
splaying the hands, hiding the feet.
Cerements I chose as for a sea crossing.
They said no shoes.

Turnip

The more you talked about the white spring turnip,
its small orb crowned with purple,
the more she came into view at the kitchen table
with hands red-raw, wielding the bread knife to perform
the daily ceremony, hacking at what she called turnips –
big, hairy, yellow *bostoons,* food fit for sows and *banbhs,*
you said

and when you conjured the perfume of the milky
moon-turnips, peppery and sweet with a hint of violet,
I saw her washing the oafish orange heads
under the cold tap, flaying them into thick slices
and boiling them up in hot water, condensation
coursing down the kitchen walls and window-panes.

Warming to your subject, you likened the difference
between the fine French navet and the rough Irish
variety to that between a thoroughbred and a dray,
and there she was again, gouging the eyes
out of fat, floury spuds and stripping giant stalks
from bottle-green cabbage leaves, the table littered
with streelish skins of onions and carrots,

and as you catalogued the lively flavours released
by the neat bulbs to a simple stew – navarin
of Spring lamb, say, with slivers of garlic, a bay leaf
and a dash of red wine – you took me only to her,
to turnip water, to its smell as she strained over the sink,
a plate clamping the pan, her hands scalded and red again
as she slapped up the stringy flesh with a dollop of butter.

Little House

In the September haze I find you
running, a child with broken shoes
haring through the smells of fern
and woodsmoke, sprinting through
the piebald sunshine, singing *Oh*
to have a little house, out of the wind
and the rain's way, flapping round
the streets and fields of Fermoy,
scooping blackberries from the hedges
and callies from the Blackwater, plucking
kindling from Glenabo, roofing apples
at Glenarousk, Coolagown, up and down
the town's hills, skipping to the pipe band's
promenade in late summer streets –
Emmet, Redmond, Clancy – in the low
gold light, fife and drum up Barrack Hill
and down the lane, the stone wall
to the iron gate, cows in the field beyond,
Nearer My God to Thee, Kilcrumper cemetery,
the sweeper at his work, brushing moss
from marble flags, and under your feet
clumps of abandoned bones waiting
for the pippin light of autumn to release
their ghosts into the sheets billowing
from the yews.

Winter Clothes

Alpine light cuts through shutters
    fixes its glare on a heap
by the door –

misery shawls of very old women
    cardigans of dust and hair
combed from floors under beds
    smocks of dirty hatching
spliced on frost-burned hedgerows –

from this mound I pick and choose
    my wear, garments too heavy to lift
seams ballasted with sweat
    casings for flesh chafed, leeched
ruched with itchy weals.

Soon I will be dragging in the streets
    freighted with drear, hem-lines adrift
threads flailing at toes and elbows
    buttons missing or straining to pop
filaments of winter soughing in disarray.

Sculptor

Camille Claudel, Paris, 1864–1943

Plaster skins peel,
fingers let eel-girls slip
from flint to shadow.

Camille at work in a blue world,
scraping ice from the river bank,
digging for earth.

Skaters cut and swivel;
flaying muscle,
she renders embrace to clay,

pulls milky limbs
from stone. Arms
lean out

to the woman
bedded among statues,
hands petrified, splitting.

Camille at work in a white world,
believing it enough to throw
flesh in plaster,

polish marble with knuckle-bone,
scorch the life of rock
with blazing eye.

City Twilight

after Baudelaire

Be quiet, my sorrow, calm down now.
You cried for night; it falls: darkness
is gathering the city in its low folds,
bringing peace to some, to others, anguish.

While the madding crowds hop and press
to pleasure's pricks, not knowing –
not caring – that the dealer will have his day,
oh sorrow, give me your hand, come away,

let them be. Look, the dead years float
their faded dresses from the balconies of the sky,
regret drifts from the river bed, smiling,

the ashen sun slumps beneath an arch
and in the east, like the slow dragging of a shroud,
listen, my love, listen to the gentle night march.

Disinherited

after Gérard de Nerval

I live in shadow – bereft – the unconsoled,
The Prince of Aquitaine in his broken tower;
My only star is dead – my jewelled lute
Bears the black sun of melancholy.

You who lay with me in my bed of earth,
Let me have Posilippo again, the Italian sea,
Flowers that eased the seal on my heart,
Gardens where rose and vine were joined.

Am I Dionysus or Apollo? A Valois lord?
My forehead is branded with a queen's kiss,
I have dreamt in the cave where the siren swims ...

Twice my soul crossed the Acheron,
Returning to make the lyre of Orpheus sing
The saint's sigh, the wraith's lamentation.

Philomel

She was running at the mouth, words
pulling in black eddies from tailbone
to fontanelle, spilling over throat walls
cords washing through red clay

crimson lake on cambric, a voice
darting unseemly threads through silk
a tongue falling on the dead land

bolting and buckling clucking and clacking
its last to the gods who turned and turned her
to a bird and still she cried jug jug on desert air

in Berkeley Square and still her song – the same
that found a path through the sad heart of Ruth –
could not be heard pining for the words
that once poured from her lips, the smiles.

Izmir

Should I happen to be visiting you in August,
Izmir, would I scuttle in the shadow of your palms,
your silk road, your velvet castle?
Would I drag in your aisles, march my tin soldiers
on your aqueduct, on your Amazonian queen,
your smeltery of races cutting and stirring
and picking on thresholds?

What are you to me that I should weep for you?
I have never seen you and yet, should I happen
to be visiting you in August, Smyrna my love,
I would kneel in your hundred houses of prayer
and know that I had knelt in all of them before,
one hundred times, paced your dark galleries,
swallowed the dust of your figs and raisins,
crept over every inch of your sea walls.

And when I had done visiting you in August,
Izmir, I would merge with your craggy panorama
at sunset and curse you, oh pearl of the Aegean.

Mahal

For you I ran ragged round India,
with bowl and stick and fraying bundle
I hauled myself through persimmon palaces.

I begged to swim out to you
at Jal Mahal, water pavilion
mired in mud.

At Chandra Mahal the moon turned
her face of ice to the pilgrim
clacking beads at the gate.

Shrieking in halls of victory and pleasure
I flew from a thousand broken windows
and, for my pains, the weeping of maharanis.

For you I fell down
India's secret wells, lugging bones
in the dark water chambers of Jaisalmer.

I was burned on the ghats at Varanasi,
came back as an elephant at Birla Mandir;
at Govind Devi, the goddess consecrated my ghost:

you had returned me to the wind,
long since my words had been snowflakes,
ashes.

My letters of love, my spectral songs,
I let them drift on the forest floors of night,
praying Krishna to let you find them

before the tiger did,
before the white mountain melted,
washing me to the Ganges.

Pastourelle

You sit in my shade
fill your face with my berries
watch nearby hills for shepherd girls
their games dancing them down
down a dust track

to where small feet will press
in warm goat tracks, where wind
crying in reeds will drive them wild
drive them into your circle
of pandemonium.

Skittish, you sit in my shade
stretching and scuffing your spine
against my skin. Passing the time.

Indigestion

I've stopped eating, just porridge and camomile tea
morning and night. I wrap myself in loose wool,
stand at the stove stirring oatmeal and grinding my teeth
and moiling over the scraping and swishing of the woman
    upstairs
hoovering her parquet floor at five in the morning.

Stirring and grinding and cutting – I have two thousand
    patches
of cloth saved for the quilts I'm going to stitch,
a thousand tea-bags collected at the corners of the earth
and two hundred shoulder pads cut from the coats of
    strangers.
The flat is crammed with jars for the birth dates of everyone
I've ever met. I never send cards.

Men don't see me now – look, look away.
I'm winter, my palette a dazzling panoply of berry reds
to push in the faces of the milk-and-watery pastel types.
I do aqua-gym, sauna, total tone, spinning
at least once a week – I've paid my membership –
and guided museum and gallery tours in four languages.

At the market I buy kilos of potatoes and pumpkins,
watch them moulder in the kitchen while I dream of soup.
Then in a fury of chopping I flay the rotting bits and pieces,
boil them to a sour puree. My sons won't touch it,
they graze from a well-stocked fridge, and are never ill.

I'm always hungry but eating gives me a pain,
bile rising in my gut, reflux pushing from colon
to epiglottis, retching in the diaphragm.
Skin of porridge lines my stomach, skin of wool
stretches over my back, shoulders, chest,
arms so thin now – the fat just fell away.

Stirring honey into bubbling pap, I swallow
a litre of camomile and at last feel – wrapped.
I could melt. Maybe I should light tapers before madonnas
in dark basilicas, join the twilight army of women
who mutter and intone, shuffle dahlias and gladioli,
polish stones.

Alter Ego

Circled by company in a downtown bar
I sense a shoe touching my shoe – surely not?
toe tipping at toe, rim of sole skimming
rim of sole, a tap-tapping in my chest.
I hold tight, hold my breath, fix my foot
in frozen intercourse with yours.

We have just met and doubtless will never
meet again but for now we are anemones
clinging to each other by rubbery suction pads
in the dark of the under-table, breathing
in unison through our crepe gills and as we do
a woman surfaces – unseen by you –

one who knows herself made for Manhattan,
knows how to take her chance, she pushes
between us, filling my shoes, pressing my foot
brazenly to yours, alive in the current as it pulses
on its short impossible circuit and is gone
even as I step onto the cold sidewalk.

Shower

Step into the hub
snap sliding doors shut
lather flannel and scrub flesh
according to an old map
hand washing furiously over shoulder
and clavicle and sternum, mindless,
half-asleep, but always scrupulous
in skirting the left breast.

A ruched scar,
left arm a sack of lymph,
every vertebra a fleck of alarm
on a bone-scanner's screen
you kept dropping the soap
trying to bend, pick it up
slap of soggy soap on wet plastic
slipping, trying to stand
banging and knocking elbows
and knees on ceramic, hot water
beating on ear drums.

In my box of steam, I go through
the morning's ablutions – neck, arm
spine from cranium to sacrum
from now till kingdom come
washing hand circling a breast
remembering you
on your knees
knowing you were through.

River in December

The grey waters lumber
through the river's womb
stirring nothing from the bed,
bringing no pebble to the shorn bank.
The grey river horse stands alone
in the lee field. Spindles poke
the sky, snag a magpie that flaps
itself free, comes in to land
on the concrete bunker
of the abandoned swimming baths.
A dirty yellow sky lowers itself
onto a scalloped lane hedged
in turf-water hatching.

Crossing

From a shaky bridge on a river
flowing west I watched
a man wading, to his thighs,
an upturned boat pitching
in olivine water. On the far bank

fiddlers played, vibrato lifting
from wood, cat's cradle swinging,
obsidian shattering to the tune
of a thousand silver heads
pulsing in synchrony.

What We Missed

Tutti li lor coperchi eran sospesi,
e fuor n'uscivan sì duri lamenti,
che ben parean di miseri e d'offesi.
—Dante, *Inferno*, Canto IX, lines 121–123

The entrance to the catacombs lies not far
from the Barrière d'Enfer – the gate to hell –
and we were waiting, on a hot August Sunday,
in a queue that snaked round the Place
Denfert Rochereau, around its fierce stone
lion, its tiny park, its cranky pigeons. For all
my familiarity with Paris, I had never been
to the underground of the dead, had only
heard tell of the stacked thigh bones,
the sweaty corridors full of the overspill
of the city's boneyards. After an hour
of squirming like sun-baked worms,
and no nearer the underworld, we turned
away …

In Arles, we managed to miss the tree-
shrouded alley of the Alyscamps, came away
without seeing the trough-like Roman tombs,
each with its head-hole – the lidless graves
that Dante was moved to put in his *Inferno*
(and out of them such harsh lamenting rose as from
a wretched and a wounded crew). We trawled
the site where the Rhone stagnates in sand,
scouring the place for monuments in grey
stone, the stone Van Gogh had turned
to wheatfield yellow – arena, amphitheatre,

Romanesque cathedral. But the Alyscamps
gave us the slip ...

I had stowed a dream of the Camargue
since childhood, a hazy image of wild white horses
tearing through the silence of a river's delta.
But when, at last, I got there, with you, the herds
were nowhere to be seen, neither galloping
in the shallows, nor cantering between palisades
of still flamingos. Green rice grass and purple sea-
lavender cooled our dust-filled eyes, and each
black fighting bull had his own white egret
standing to attention on his shoulder.
But the salt-washed horses of my child-fancy
had been tamed, were trotting in lines
along the sand, with helmeted children
on their backs.

Goodbye Sounds Like This

Two people said goodbye to me today.

The first, my lover, on the phone, said byebye –
rapid fire, sudden death, bullet between the eyes.
And each time he says byebye in that cut-you-off-
like-a-rasher way I make a mental note to beg him
to contrive another way of taking his leave,
to bypass the phone moment when all the years of –
what? – come crowding into his voice, making him
end with the coldest and cleanest of Queen's Counsel
cut-glass cutlass byebyes, the blade of the receiver
slamming, sending me spinning, snipped
from the telephonic thread.

The second, my father, suddenly old on my doorstep,
kissed me on the cheek and headed off down
the path. Then, turning on his heel,
he threw the farewell word over his shoulder
and as a syllable flew out to meet the one
that had gone before something snapped
and Eurydice was tumbling backward
through air, spinning down to the shadows
and Orpheus was stretching out his arm,
a strangled note her only way of reaching
him, and not a thing he could do to save her.

Two Beds

Blood gone, sheets washed, dried, on bed –
his text, sent four days later, made her eyes
dart round her place, the dog's dinner
of bed-linen the three pillows giving her a crick
in her neck the powdered sugar of Turkish Delight
dusting a side table the wine bottles (Marescialla,
Morellino di Scansano) crammed against the back
door the prawn shells that had torn her fingers spilling
over the bottom of the garden the shards of glass
on the bathroom floor the second picture that fell
from the wall his books on the bed under the bed
greeting her from the dark hallway every night now
for nineteen nights – she closed her eyes, saw him
neat, between crisp sheets.

Long Distance

You sit on the balcony, sip
iced coffee and watermelon juice,
watch water taxis zip by
to the palm islands, the white sail
of the skyscraper hotel billowing
across the bay, palms standing
stock still. Mynah birds chatter
under latticed arches, the sun
slips into water, blood-red light
breaks across the delta. All this
you watch from your balcony
of mirrored marble and cane.
I open shutters to a blast of white,
late-blooming snow furring
the newly-budded cherry blossom.
There's a quick March stab in the air.
Robins do their frenzied dance,
digging for grubs, a renegade blackbird
hops valiantly across frozen grass.
The morning yawns, its jaws tear
up the garden, the planet, tipping
me into the crack that opens.

New Year's Day

Perhaps that's what brought us together: our dogdom.

Two strays in the street below sniff at a life-belt,
sacrifice to last night's revels. Cars stalled at the lights
have their hair of ice scraped back to let boy riders
glimpse the frozen river. Gulls are pirouetting backwards
down the black stream, white faces looking west,
bodies bobbing eastward on the polar wind.

Across the river, the powder-blue Palladian facade
of Atkins Garden Centre, all arched and trellised,
is flush with ice vines. Overhead, a perished full moon
is floating in a blessed pool of melt-water
visible through a crack in the ice of the night
sky – a Christmas quail's egg suspended in aspic.

A swan has flown in from the lough, settles
in the shadows of the Christy Ring bridge.
White wings are flapping on the footpath – a dead bird
soldered to frozen stone, or a paper napkin blown
from some New Year's party? Here, in the Eastern Tandoori
the indigo candle is spluttering out, the air is alight
with cardamom and cumin and the sitar is crying please
please let us stay here forever.

Beyond the window, one of the mongrels slopes along
the quay wall, snapping at the shoals of white flecks
drifting down-river.

Hi-Lili Hi-Lo

A song of love is a sad song
hi-lili hi-lili hi-lo –
but here we go travelling
the world, tracking ghosts
through forests, listening for birds,
for what their songs might tell us
of the one, the only – Hurry up! Hurry up!
This beast has fangs and will
gobble you! Let us go waltzing,
my love, where sticks are sharp
and shadows numberless, where
to look away is to lose your love
forever. Sing me a song of graves
opened again, of the dead lifted
into the arms of the living.
Take my hand, pull me down
to the wet ground where you are
rolling, hold me in your arms,
let me roar into the drains
for our lost children. Safety pins
will fall from the waist-bands
of old men, showering us
with spiky kisses. Let us sing
a song, our very own –
a song of love is a song of woe,
don't ask me how I know.
Hi-lili hi-lili hi-lo –

Oracle Bone

in the China room of the British Museum

The shoulder of a cow,
translucent as very old skin,
is offered to the eye
in a glass tomb. Soldiering
bone – rotator hauling
the plough, trammelling
earth, harnessed to the wheel,
to the grinding stone –
and, pared of flesh, a blade,
a pillow for the tired head,
a cup for tears, a slate
where priests scratched,
read divinations in cracks,
bone splintering to the tune
of burning wires, thrumming
with the voices of ancestors.

The oracle bone keeps
the company of objects unearthed –
tiny mountain worlds in balsam,
tail-less and mane-less horses
and their grooms, glazed
in the gloomy greens
and browns of mineral dyes,
bottles robed in the sap
of lacquer trees, long-necked
ceramic jars that once lay
in the cool river, jade discs
that sealed the mouths of the dead,

sandstone ears of bodhisattvas,
disciples stalled just short of Nirvana,
tuned to the cries of the world.

Somewhere Else

it's a cold Spring, three cormorants
are flying in, maybe, to huddle on a
rainy weir, but here, at the Wednesday
market, it's fat strawberries from the *garrigue*
and golden onions with wild green hair
and inky octopus lolling on reefs of scarlet
bell peppers. Through dapple-dapple lime-
green freckles flickering on piebald bark
and limestone clock-towers and fountains
we drive, stopping at the sign of the scallop-
shell of Saint James to drink the citrus wine
and eat the sweet oysters of Bouzigues.
In the streets of Sète, a seagull presents
himself at locked glass doors – knock,
wait, hop on, dome-headed pilgrim!
Are you looking for your mate? She's been
snared in nets, bamboozled by the oysters,
the lake's slinky contortionists, shimmering
under water on their salty daisy chains.
Gull cries follow us. Somewhere else,
three cormorants are raising a black flag
above an icy river.

* *garrigue:* scrubland in the Mediterranean region

What's Left

with thanks to Leonard Cohen and Gustave Courbet

I carried it round all summer on scraps
of worn paper, in various bags, on trains,
on two planes, feeling it had the makings

of something but now the moment has come
I cannot lay my hands on the damned thing,
it has flowered without me, complete

in its vanishing act, leaving me never to know
what it was that made me cling to its threads –
was it a coded journal of a man on a broken hill

silhouette against a mackerel sky, in a wet Dublin field,
calling to someone in a crowd to dance him
through curtains that kisses have outworn

promising to raise a tent of shelter,
though every thread is torn – or a secret history
of goats lolling in foxgloves on a cliff's edge

and long grasses rolling in waves with the breeze
from the north harbour on Cape Clear – or a red prayer flag
for the rain, the endless summer rain falling

on Fitzgerald's Park, on the piles of sweating rose petals,
on the sleek stone boy in the lily pond – is he pulling a thorn
from the sole of his foot? – or a bird note book

full of the spindly egrets wading in the salt marshes
between Narbonne and Perpignan, seen from a train,
the heavy bodies of gulls lumbering above the tile roofs
of a Mediterranean graveyard?

What remains of my calendar of rain and burning blue,
my portrait of a man standing on a rock, saluting,
with his hat, the vast emptiness of the waves,
asking to be lifted, like an olive-branch?